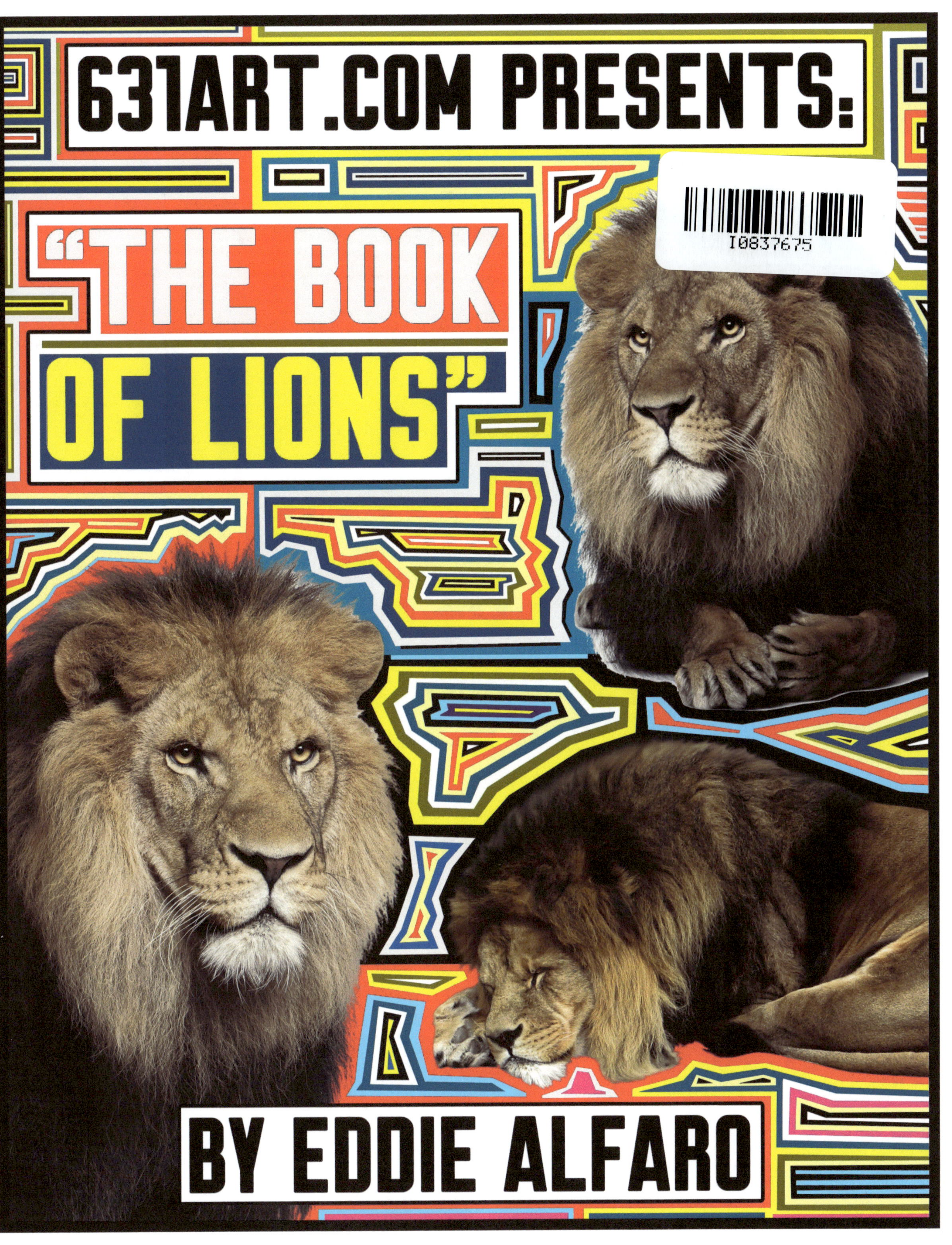

631ART.COM PRESENTS:
"THE BOOK OF LIONS"
I0837675
BY EDDIE ALFARO

THE HEAVIEST LION ON
RECORD WEIGHED AN
AMAZING 826 LB.

LIONS HAVE ROUND PUPILS, INSTEAD OF VERTICAL SLITS THAT ARE FOUND IN DOMESTIC CATS.

LIONS ARE THE MOST SOCIAL
MEMBER OF THE CAT FAMILY
AND LIVES IN PRIDES OF UP
TO 25+ INDIVIDUALS.

LIONS ENGAGE IN
COMPLEX COMMUNICATION,
THEY ROAR, GRUNT,
MOAN, GROWL, SNARL,
MEOW, PURR, HUM,
PUFF AND WOOF.

A LION CAN RUN FOR SHORT DISTANCES
AT 50 MPH AND LEAP AS FAR AS 36 FEET.

THE NAME FOR LION IN SWAHILI,
AN AFRICAN LANGUAGE, IS 'SIMBA'.

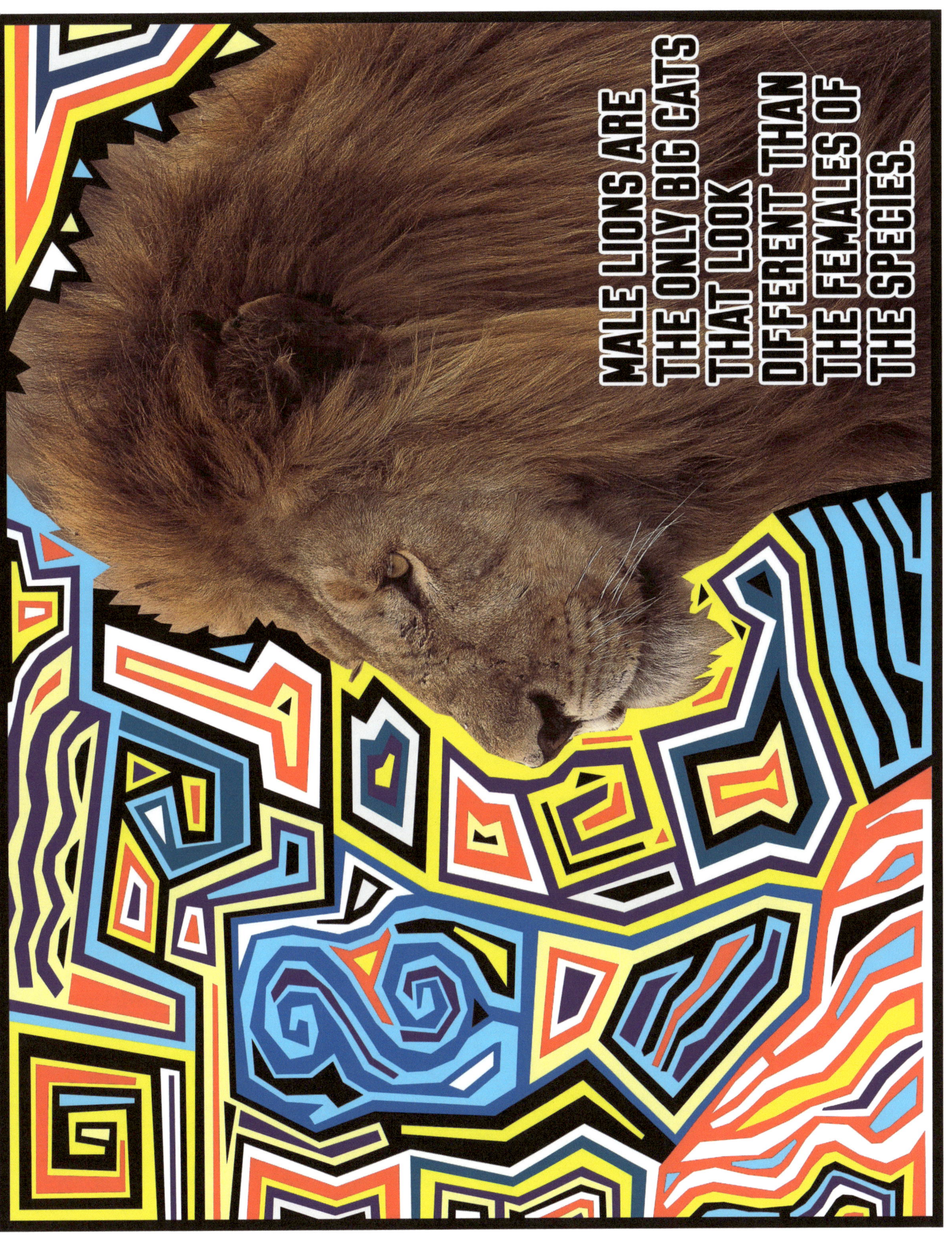
MALE LIONS ARE
THE ONLY BIG CATS
THAT LOOK
DIFFERENT THAN
THE FEMALES OF
THE SPECIES.

FEMALE LIONS
PREFER TO MATE
WITH MALES THAT
HAVE THE LONGEST
AND DARKEST MANES.

ASLAN IS THE TURKISH AND MONGOLIAN WORD FOR "LION."
IT IS ALSO THE NAME OF THE LION IN C. S. LEWIS' "THE CHRONICLES OF NARNIA."

ALTHOUGH THE LION IS KNOWN AS "THE KING OF THE JUNGLE," LIONS DO NOT LIVE IN JUNGLES. THEY LIVE ONLY IN GRASSLANDS AND PLAINS.

TWO OR MORE LIONESSES IN A GROUP TEND TO GIVE BIRTH AROUND THE SAME TIME, AND THE CUBS ARE RAISED TOGETHER.

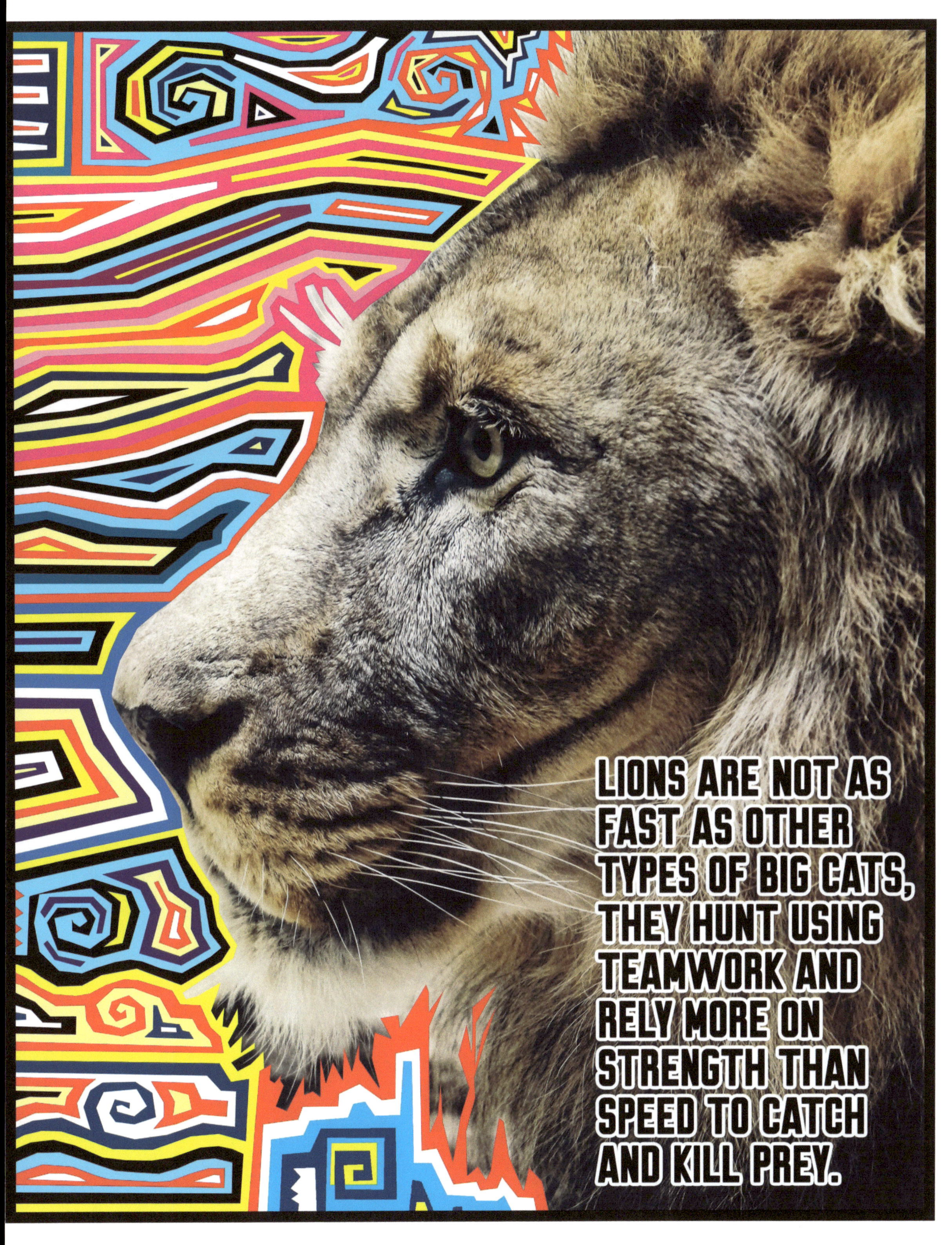
LIONS ARE NOT AS
FAST AS OTHER
TYPES OF BIG CATS,
THEY HUNT USING
TEAMWORK AND
RELY MORE ON
STRENGTH THAN
SPEED TO CATCH
AND KILL PREY.

LIONS CAN SEE
SIX TIMES BETTER
IN THE DARK
THAN A HUMAN.

UNLIKE MOST OTHER CATS, LIONS ARE GREAT SWIMMERS.

A PRIDE'S TERRITORY MAY INCLUDE
UP TO 100 SQUARE MILES.

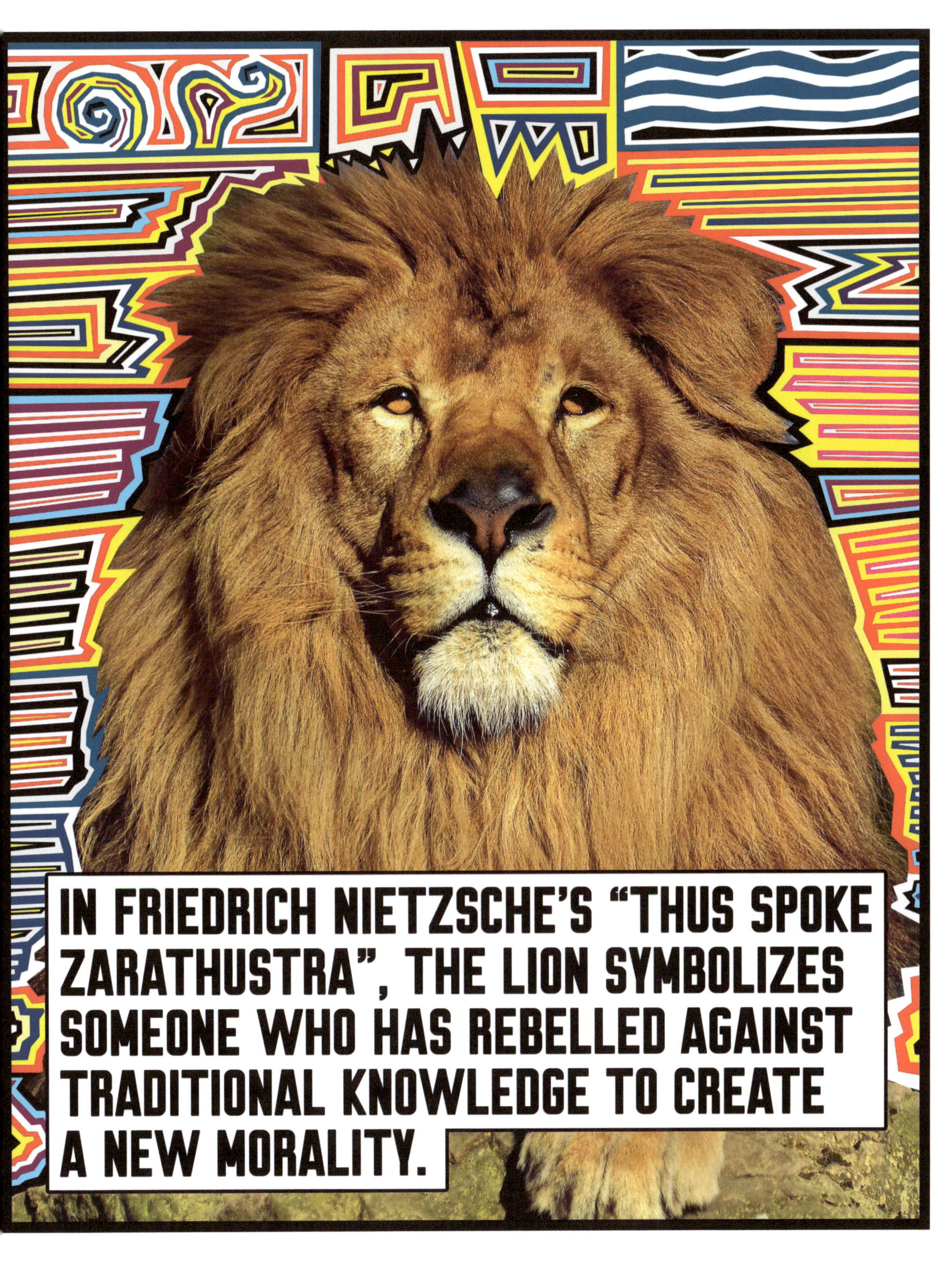

IN FRIEDRICH NIETZSCHE'S "THUS SPOKE ZARATHUSTRA", THE LION SYMBOLIZES SOMEONE WHO HAS REBELLED AGAINST TRADITIONAL KNOWLEDGE TO CREATE A NEW MORALITY.

FEMALE LIONS ARE MAINLY THE HUNTERS OF THE PRIDE, WHILE MALES ONLY HUNT WHEN A BIG KILL IS INVOLVED.

LIONS DO NOT PURR. THE ONLY MEMBER OF THE BIG CAT FAMILY THAT DOES IS THE LEOPARD.

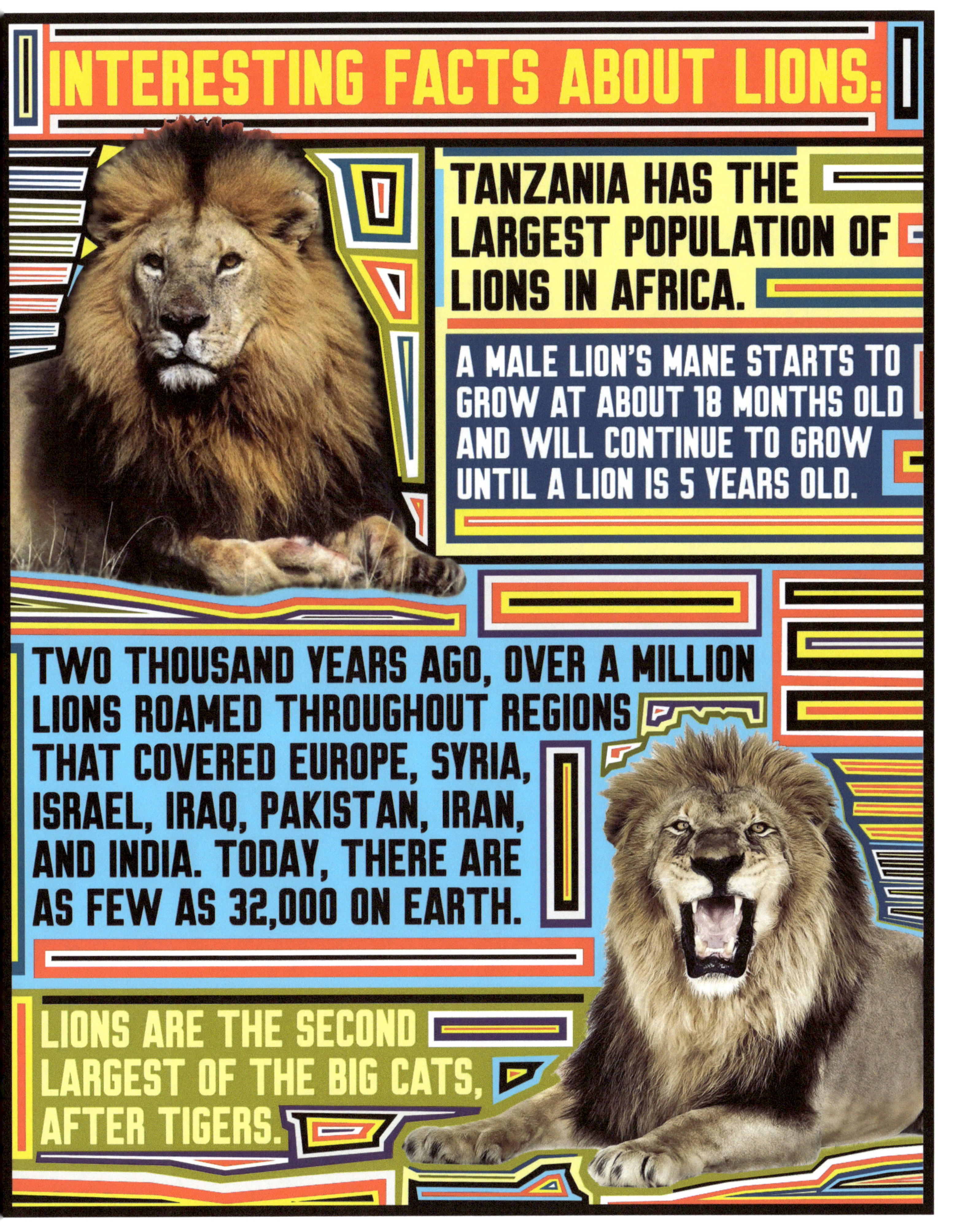

INTERESTING FACTS ABOUT LIONS:

TANZANIA HAS THE LARGEST POPULATION OF LIONS IN AFRICA.

A MALE LION'S MANE STARTS TO GROW AT ABOUT 18 MONTHS OLD AND WILL CONTINUE TO GROW UNTIL A LION IS 5 YEARS OLD.

TWO THOUSAND YEARS AGO, OVER A MILLION LIONS ROAMED THROUGHOUT REGIONS THAT COVERED EUROPE, SYRIA, ISRAEL, IRAQ, PAKISTAN, IRAN, AND INDIA. TODAY, THERE ARE AS FEW AS 32,000 ON EARTH.

LIONS ARE THE SECOND LARGEST OF THE BIG CATS, AFTER TIGERS.

THE DARKER A MALE LION'S MANE IS, THE OLDER HE IS.
A MALE LION CAN STRETCH UP TO 10 FEET LONG AND WEIGH 400–500 POUNDS.
A LION'S BITE IS 30 TIMES STRONGER THAN THE BITE OF A HOUSECAT.
THEY ACTUALLY HAVE THE WEAKEST BITE OF ALL THE BIG CATS. THE JAGUAR HAS THE STRONGEST BITE FORCE OF ANY BIG CAT
THE MOST DANGEROUS LAND ANIMAL IN AFRICA IS NOT THE LION BUT THE HIPPOPOTAMUS.

LIONS HUNT MOSTLY AT NIGHT AND HAVE ABOUT A 50% SUCCESS RATE.

LIONS COME IN SEVERAL DIFFERENT COLORS, INCLUDING TAN, BROWN, YELLOW, AND EVEN RED.

A MALE LION'S MANE STARTS TO GROW AT ABOUT 18 MONTHS OLD AND WILL CONTINUE TO GROW UNTIL A LION IS 5 YEARS OLD.

THE FAMOUS MGM LION IS NAMED "LEO THE LION" AND HAS OPENED EVERY ONE OF ITS MOVIES SINCE 1929.

THANK YOU.
THE END.

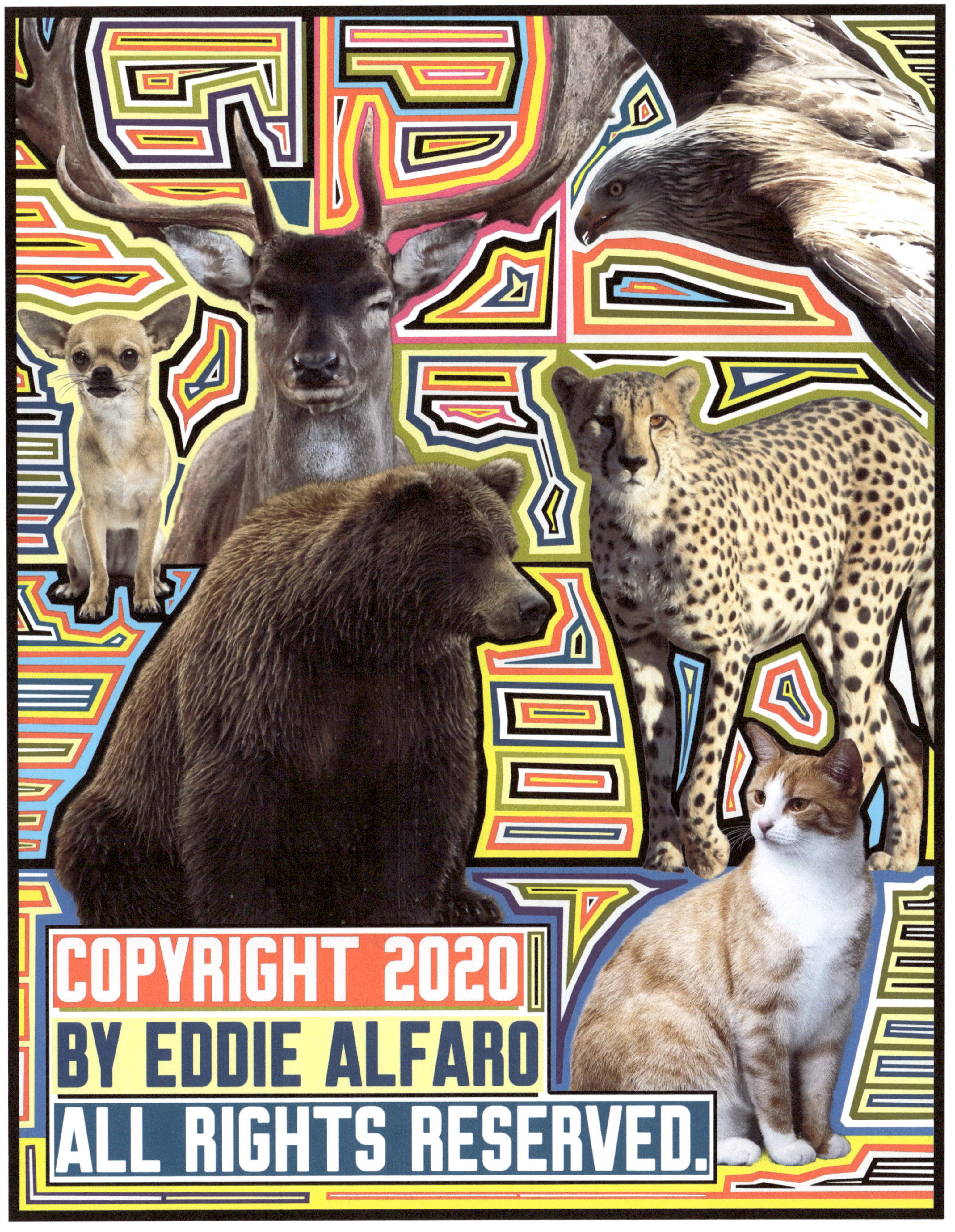
COPYRIGHT 2020
BY EDDIE ALFARO
ALL RIGHTS RESERVED.

MORE BOOKS AT:

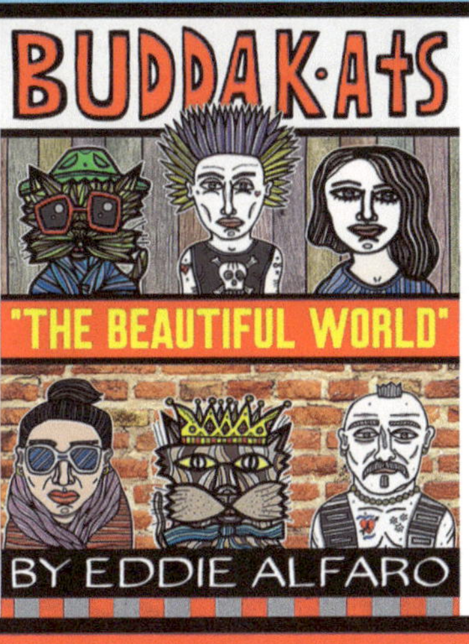

631ART.COM

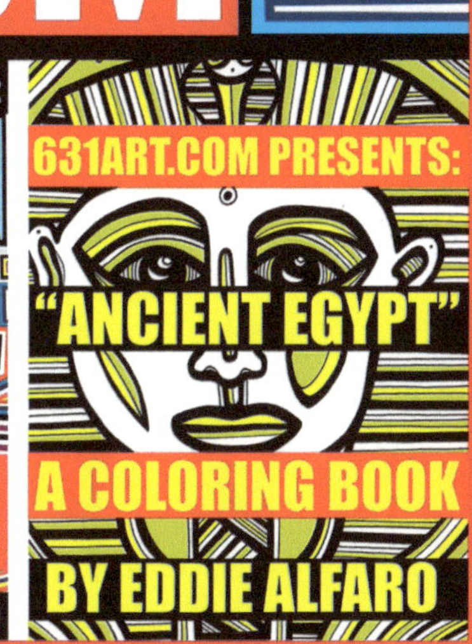